MY FIRST BOOK ABOUT

TEXAS

by Carole Marsh

This activity book has material which correlates with the Texas Essential Knowledge and Skills. At every opportunity, we have tried to relate information to the History and Social Science, English, Science, Math, Civics, Economics, and Computer Technology TEKS directives. For additional information, go to our websites: **www.texasexperience.com** or **www.gallopade.com**.

Winner of the
2002 Learning Magazine  Teacher's Choice Award

Gallopade is proud to be a member of the National Council for the Social Studies, as well as these educational organizations and associations:

The Texas Experience Series

The Texas Experience Paperback Book!

My First Pocket Guide to Texas!

The Big Texas Reproducible Activity Book

The Totally Texas Coloring Book!

My First Book About Texas!

Texas "Jography!": A Fun Run Through Our State

Texas Jeopardy: Answers & Questions About Our State

The Texas Experience Sticker Pack

The Texas Experience! Poster/Map

Discover Texas CD-ROM

Texas "GEO" Bingo Game

Texas "HISTO" Bingo Game

A Word... From the Author

Do you know when I think children should start learning about their very own state? When they're born! After all, even when you're a little baby, this is your state too! This is where you were born. Even if you move away, this will always be your "home state." And if you were not born here, but moved here—this is still your state as long as you live here.

We know people love their country. Most people are very patriotic. We fly the U.S. flag. We go to Fourth of July parades. But most people also love their state. Our state is like a mini-country to us. We care about its places and people and history and flowers and birds.

As a child, we learn about our little corner of the world. Our room. Our home. Our yard. Our street. Our neighborhood. Our town. Even our county.

But very soon, we realize that we are part of a group of neighbor towns that make up our great state! Our newspaper carries stories about our state. The TV news is about happenings in our state. Our state's sports teams are our favorites. We are proud of our state's main tourist attractions.

From a very young age, we are aware that we are a part of our state. This is where our parents pay taxes and vote and where we go to school. BUT, we usually do not get to study about our state until we are in school for a few years!

So, this book is an introduction to our great state. It's just for you right now. Why wait to learn about your very own state? It's an exciting place and reading about it now will give you a head start for that time when you "officially" study our state history! Enjoy,

Carole Marsh

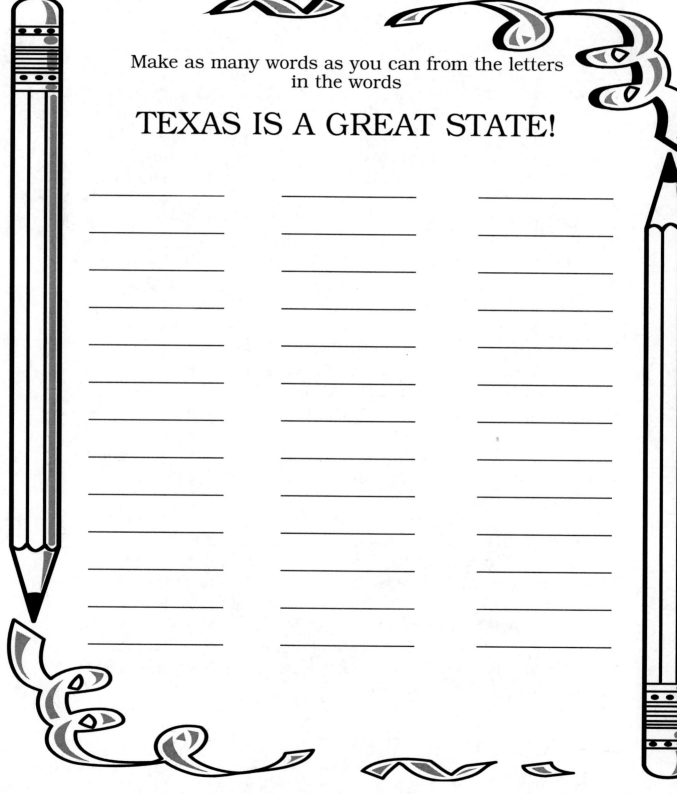

Texas
Let's Have Words!

Make as many words as you can from the letters
in the words

TEXAS IS A GREAT STATE!

Texas
The 28th State

Do you know when Texas became a state? Texas became the 28th state in 1845.

Color Texas red. Color the Atlantic and Pacific Oceans blue. Color the rest of the U.S. states shown here green.

Pacific Ocean

Atlantic Ocean

TX

Texas
State Flag

Do you feel proud when you see the Texas state flag flying high overhead? Texas has a red, white, and blue flag. The left one-third of the flag is a blue vertical stripe with a lone white star in the center. The right two-thirds has a single white horizontal stripe atop a single red horizontal stripe. Red represents bravery, white stands for strength, and blue symbolizes loyalty. The flag was adopted in 1839.

Color the Texas flag below.

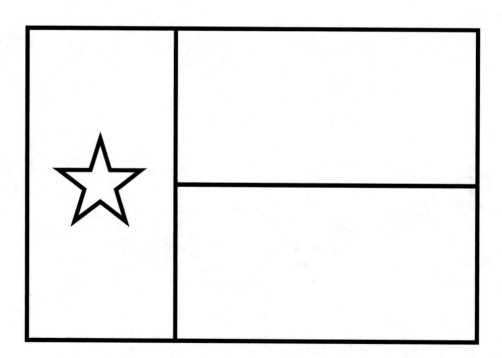

HI, FRIEND!

Texas
State Bird

Most states have a state bird. It reminds us that we should "fly high" to achieve our goals. The Texas state bird is the Mockingbird. Mockingbirds are songbirds that live in open country and farmlands.

Circle your state bird, then color all the birds.

THE EARLY BIRD GETS THE WORM!

FINCH

MOCKINGBIRD

ROBIN

BLUE JAY

EAGLE

CARDINAL

Texas
State Seal and Motto

The Texas state seal consists of a star of five points, encircled by olive and live oak branches, and the words "The State of Texas." Texas' state motto is: *Friendship.*

In 25 words or less, explain what the state motto means:

_____

_____

_____

_____

Color the state seal.

HOLA, AMIGO!

Texas
State Flower

Every state has a favorite flower. The Texas state flower is the Bluebonnet.

The Bluebonnet is a plant with compound leaves and clusters of blue flowers.

Color the picture of our state flower.

Texas
State Tree

Our state tree reminds us that our roots should run deep if we want to grow straight and tall! The state tree for Texas is the Pecan. The Pecan can be found in the southern U.S. It is a tree with furrowed bark and edible nuts.

Finish drawing the Pecan Tree, then color it.

Texas
State Fish

Guadalupe Bass
Micropterus Salmoides

The Texas state fish is a member of the sunfish family and black bass group of fish.

Draw 6 fish in the water below. Color each one a different color.

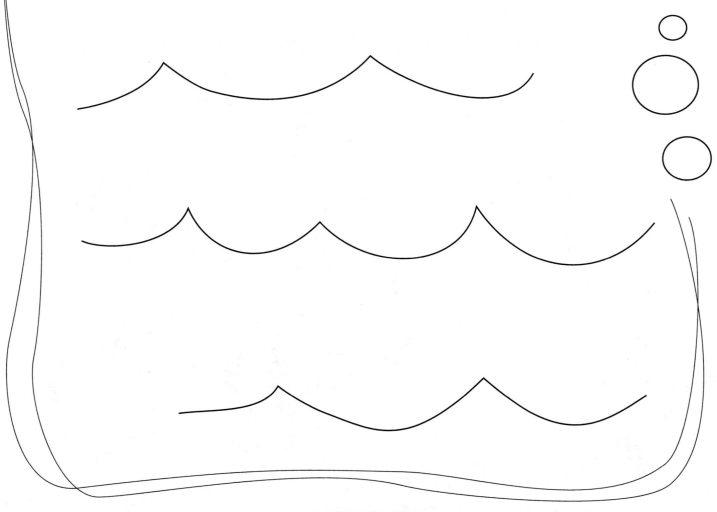

Texas
State Explorers

The first recorded exploration of today's Texas was made in the 1530s by Alvar Núñez Cabeza de Vaca. In 1540, Francisco Vázquez de Coronado crossed the High Plains of Texas. Louis Moscosco de Alvarado ventured as far west as central Texas in 1542. La Salle established Fort Saint Louis on the Texas coast in 1684.

Color the things an explorer might have used.

LET'S GO EXPLORING!

Latin, hey?

Texas
State Insect

Monarch Butterfly
Danaus Plexippus

A Monarch Butterfly has large, colorful wings and small front legs.

The Monarch Butterfly's wingspan is about 4 inches.

Put an X by the insects that are <u>not</u> a Monarch Butterfly and then color all the critters!

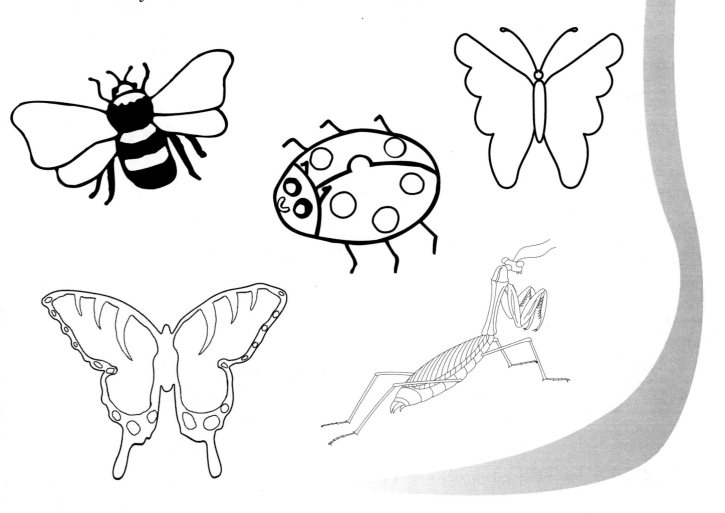

One Day I Can Vote!

When you are 18 and register according to state laws - you can vote! So please do! Your vote counts!

You are running for a class office.

You get 41 votes!

Here is your opponent!

He gets 16 votes!

ANSWER THE FOLLOWING QUESTIONS:

1. Who won? ❑ you ❑ your opponent

2. How many votes were cast altogether?

3. How many votes did the winner win by?

Texas
State Capital

The state capital of Texas is Austin. Add your town to the map. Now add other towns you have visited to the map. (CHECK & SEE IF YOU SPELLED THEM CORRECTLY!)

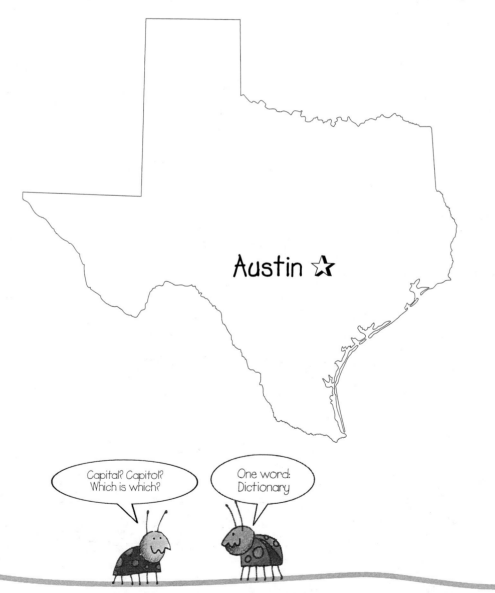

Austin ☆

Capital? Capitol? Which is which?

One word: Dictionary

Texas
Governor

The governor of Texas is our state's leader.
Do some research to complete the biography of our governor.

Governor's name:
_____

Paste a picture of the governor in the box.

The governor was born in this state:
_____

The governor has been in office since:
_____

Names of the governor's family members:
_____
_____
_____

Interesting facts about the governor:
_____
_____
_____
_____
_____
_____

Texas
Crops

Some families in our state make their living from the land.

Some of our state's crops and agricultural products are:

WORD BANK

corn	peanuts	wheat
cotton	pecans	rice

UNSCRAMBLE THESE IMPORTANT STATE CROPS

ahtwe _____   rnco _____

npsuate _____   necaps _____

toncot _____   cire _____

Texas
State Holidays

Martin Luther King Day - third Monday in January
Texas Independence Day - March 2
San Jacinto Day April 21
Emancipation Day - June 19
Lyndon B. Johnson's birthday - August 27

Number these holidays in order from the beginning of the year.

Columbus Day 2nd Monday in October	Thanksgiving 4th Thursday in November	Presidents' Day 3rd Monday in February
Independence July 4	Martin Luther King, Jr. Day 3rd Monday in January	New Year's Day January 1
Memorial Day last Monday in May	Veterans Day November 11	Christmas December 25

Texas
Nickname

Texas has a nickname! The state nickname is "The Lone Star State." The nickname arose from the state flag, which symbolizes an independent republic fighting for its freedom.

What other nicknames would suit our state and why?

_____

_____

_____

_____

_____

_____

_____

_____

_____

_____

_____

How BIG is Our State?

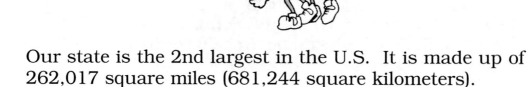

Our state is the 2nd largest in the U.S. It is made up of 262,017 square miles (681,244 square kilometers).

Can you answer the following questions?

1. How many states are there in the United States?

    _____

2. This many states are smaller than our state:

    _____

3. This many states are larger than our state:

    _____

4. One mile = 5,280 ____ ____ ____ ____

    HINT:

5. Draw a picture of a "square" mile below:

BIGFOOT WAS HERE!

Answers: 1-50; 2-48; 3-1; 4-feet

Texas
People

A state is not just towns and mountains and rivers. A state is its people! But the really important people in a state are not always famous. You may know them—they may be your mom, your dad, or your teacher. The average, everyday person is the one who makes the state a good state. How? By working hard, by paying taxes, by voting, and by helping Texas children grow up to be good state citizens!

Match each Texas person with their accomplishment.

1. Gene Autrey

2. Earl Campbell

3. Dwight Eisenhower

4. Oveta Hobby

5. Buddy Holly

6. Scott Joplin

7. Katherine Porter

8. Chester Nimitz

9. Babe Zaharias

A. Olympic track and field gold medalist

B. commander of the Pacific Fleet during World War II

C. writer, Pulitzer Prize winner

D. social reformer, publisher

E. singer, musician

F. singer, actor, baseball team owner

G. pro football player

H. 34th U.S. president

I. musician, founder of ragtime

Answers: 1-F; 2-G; 3-H; 4-D; 5-E; 6-I; 7-C; 8-B; 9-A

Texas
Gazetteer

A gazetteer is a list of places. Use the word bank to complete the names of some of these famous places in our state:

1. D_L _A_

2. SA _ AN_ _NIO

3. F_R_ W_ _TH

4. R_ _ GR _N_E

5. HO_S_ _N

6. CHI_ _A_UAN D_S_RT

7. B_G _E N_

8. T_E _LAM_

9. TH _ P_ _HA_ _LE

10. _U_ _ O_ M_X I_O

WORD BANK

The Panhandle
Big Bend
San Antonio
Gulf of Mexico
Dallas

The Alamo
Houston
Chihuahuan
Desert
Fort Worth
Rio Grande

Texas
Neighbors

No person or state lives alone. You have neighbors where you live. Sometimes they may be right next door. Other times, they may be way down the road. But you live in the same neighborhood and are interested in what goes on there.

You have neighbors at school. The children who sit in front, beside, or behind you are your neighbors. You may share books. You might borrow a pencil. They might ask you to move so they can see the board better.

We have a lot in common with our state neighbors. Some of our land is alike. We share some history. We care about our part of the country. We share borders. Some of our people go there; some of their people come here. Most of the time we get along with our state neighbors. Even when we argue or disagree, it is a good idea for both of us to work it out. After all, states are not like people—they can't move away!

Use the color key to color Texas and its neighbors.

Color Key:

Texas–purple
Louisiana–red
Oklahoma–blue
New Mexico–green
Mexico–yellow
Arkansas–orange

The highest point in the state is Guadalupe Peak. Guadalupe Peak is 8,751 feet (2,667 meters) above sea level.

Draw a picture of Guadalupe Peak.

The lowest point in the state is on the Texas coast. The Texas coast is at sea level.

Draw a picture of the Texas coast.

Texas
Old Man River

Texas has many great rivers. Rivers give us water for our crops. Rivers are also water "highways." On these water highways travel crops, manufactured goods, people, and many other things—including children in tire tubes!

Here are some of Texas' most important rivers:

SABINE	RIO GRANDE	RED
CANADIAN	PECOS	TRINITY
SAN ANTONIO	BRAZOS	GUADALUPE

Draw a kid "tubing" down a Texas River!

Weather ... Or Not!

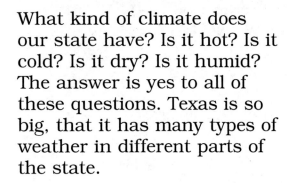

What kind of climate does our state have? Is it hot? Is it cold? Is it dry? Is it humid? The answer is yes to all of these questions. Texas is so big, that it has many types of weather in different parts of the state.

You might think adults talk about the weather a lot. But our state's weather is very important to us. Crops need water and sunshine. Weather can affect the tourist industry. Good weather can mean more money for our state. Bad weather can cause problems that cost money.

ACTIVITY: Do you watch the nightly news at your house? If you do, you might see the weather report. Tonight, tune in the weather report. The reporter often talks about our state's regions, cities and towns, and our neighboring states. Watching the weather report is a great way to learn about our state. It also helps you know what to wear to school tomorrow!

What is the weather outside now? Draw a picture.

Texas
Indian Tribes

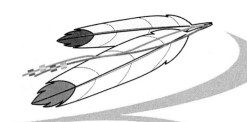

The American Indians were first on our land, long before it was a state. Texas' main Indian tribes include:

CADDO	ALABAMA-COUSHATTA
ATAKAPANS	APACHÉ
TIWA	KICKAPOO

Help Maize find her way through the maize (corn) field maze to her hut made of saplings!

Texas
Website Page

Here is a website you can go to and learn more about Texas:
www.state.tx.us

Design your own state website page on the computer screen below.

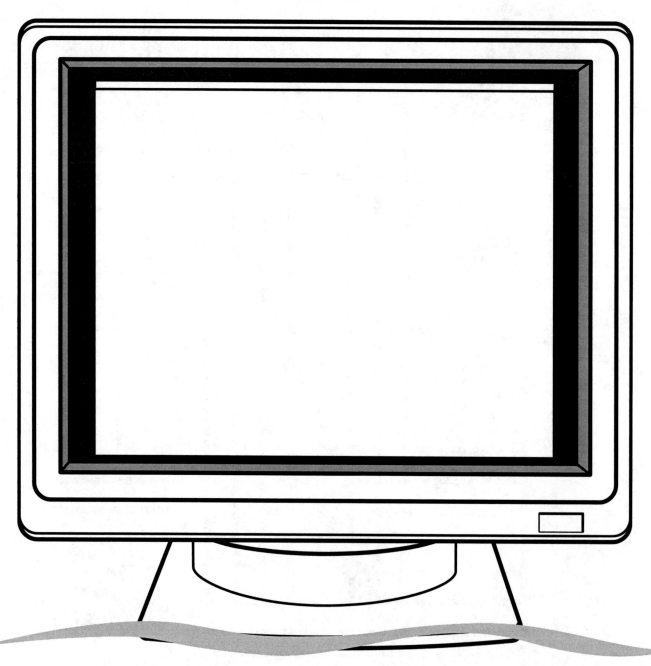

Texas
Regions

Our state is divided into regions. When we are little, our state seems very big to us. We wonder how people drive around it and not get lost. We wonder how we can learn about a whole state. Guess what? Bigger children—(and even adults)—wonder the same thing! Do you know how to make a job easier? Right! Divide it into smaller parts.

Every state has different regions. A state is usually divided into sections that have something in common. The most common thing that a part of a state might have is its geography. It may be mountainous. It may be by the ocean. Texas has four main regions. They are:

GULF COASTAL PLAINS
GREAT PLAINS
CENTRAL PLAINS
MOUNTAINS AND BASINS

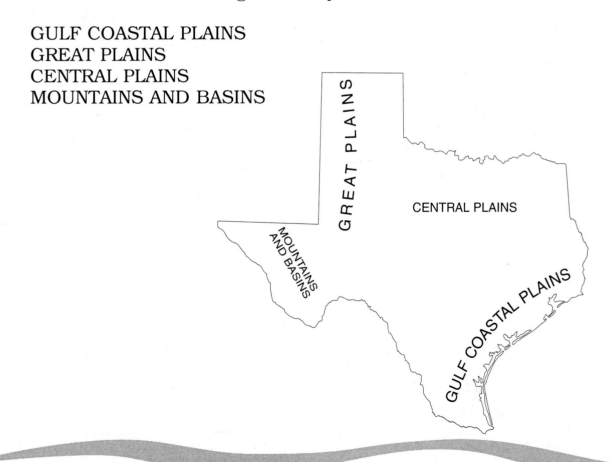

State Song

Here is the first verse of our state song:

TITLE: *Texas, Our Texas.*

VERSE 1:

Texas, our Texas! All hail the mighty State!
Texas, our Texas! so wonderful, so great!
Boldest and grandest, withstanding every test;
O empire wide and glorious, you stand supremely
blest.

God bless you, Texas! And keep you brave and strong,
That you may grow in power and worth, throughout
the ages long.

NOW, WRITE A SECOND VERSE!

_____

_____

_____

_____

_____

_____

Texas
Spelling Bee!

What's All The Buzz About?

Here are some words related to your state. See if you can find them in the Word Search below.

WORD LIST

STATE	RIVER	PEOPLE	TREE	BIRD
FLAG	VOTE	FLOWER	SONG	BAY

```
A  X  N  Y  H  N  S  S  D  G  T  R  E  P
V  O  T  E  M  A  O  S  E  H  B  A  Y  E
S  N  B  R  X  B  N  K  S  X  B  D  S  O
Y  B  P  Q  L  S  G  N  G  R  I  J  X  P
R  I  V  E  R  P  P  L  R  T  Y  U  E  L
Q  R  E  R  T  Y  Z  E  E  R  T  O  T  E
R  D  P  P  A  H  A  O  N  E  C  K  A  R
S  X  E  G  H  B  J  C  P  W  E  R  B  I
P  O  B  U  Y  U  Y  H  E  O  L  L  D  O
Q  U  F  L  A  G  R  K  R  L  X  Z  L  P
Z  X  R  D  G  H  R  E  U  F  L  L  A  L
M  R  D  W  Q  N  M  N  S  T  A  T  E  Z
```

Texas
Trivia

The last battle of the Civil War was fought at Palmito Ranch, near Brownsville.

Texas is the nation's leader in the production of cotton, cattle, sheep, wool, natural gas, oil, salt, and sulphur.

Texas was its own country for 10 years before it became a state.

Texas is one of many states whose name was taken from an Indian word. *Tejas* is a Caddo word that means "Friend."

Texas has had 6 national flags flying over it: those of Spain, France, Mexico, the Republic of Texas, the Confederacy, and the U.S.

Texas legally can split itself into five states, if it wants to, under the terms of its annexation agreement.

Texas has the most drive-in theaters of any state.

In Texas, it was once illegal for a man to carry a pair of pliers.

Oil was first struck near Corsicana in 1894.

Many people like to visit Texas. They think it is a beautiful state and love the historic places, the beautiful scenery, and our friendly people.

Add another fact that you know here:_____